This Messy Entertainment book belongs to:

. . . .

. . . .

Published By Messy Entertainment Ltd 2017
ISBN 978-1-9998015-0-2
Messy Entertainment Ltd
www.messyentertainment.com

The Shallows Of The Sea - Jellyfish 2017 © Messy Entertainment Ltd
All rights reserved.

This book or any portion thereof may not be reproduced or used
in any manner whatsoever without the express written permission
of the publisher except for the use of brief quotations in a book review.

ALL ABOUT ME...

Jellyfish

- Thousands of species of jellyfish are alive today
- Some of us can glow in the dark, how cool is that!
- Jellyfish have been around for millions of years
- We do not have a heart, a brain or any bones
- We like to eat small plants, fish, shrimps and crabs

We live in all the oceans on Earth and we can be found in shallow or deep water

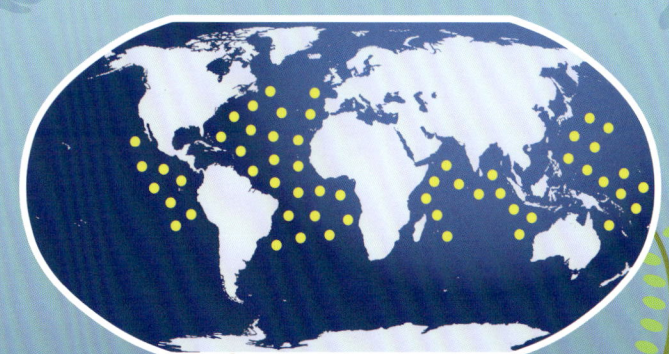

Conservation Status

- Critically Endangered
- Endangered
- Vulnerable
- Near Threatened
- Least Concerned

There are thousands of jellyfish species. Most are concidered not to be endangered in 2017.

Jellyfish

How many jellyfish can you count?

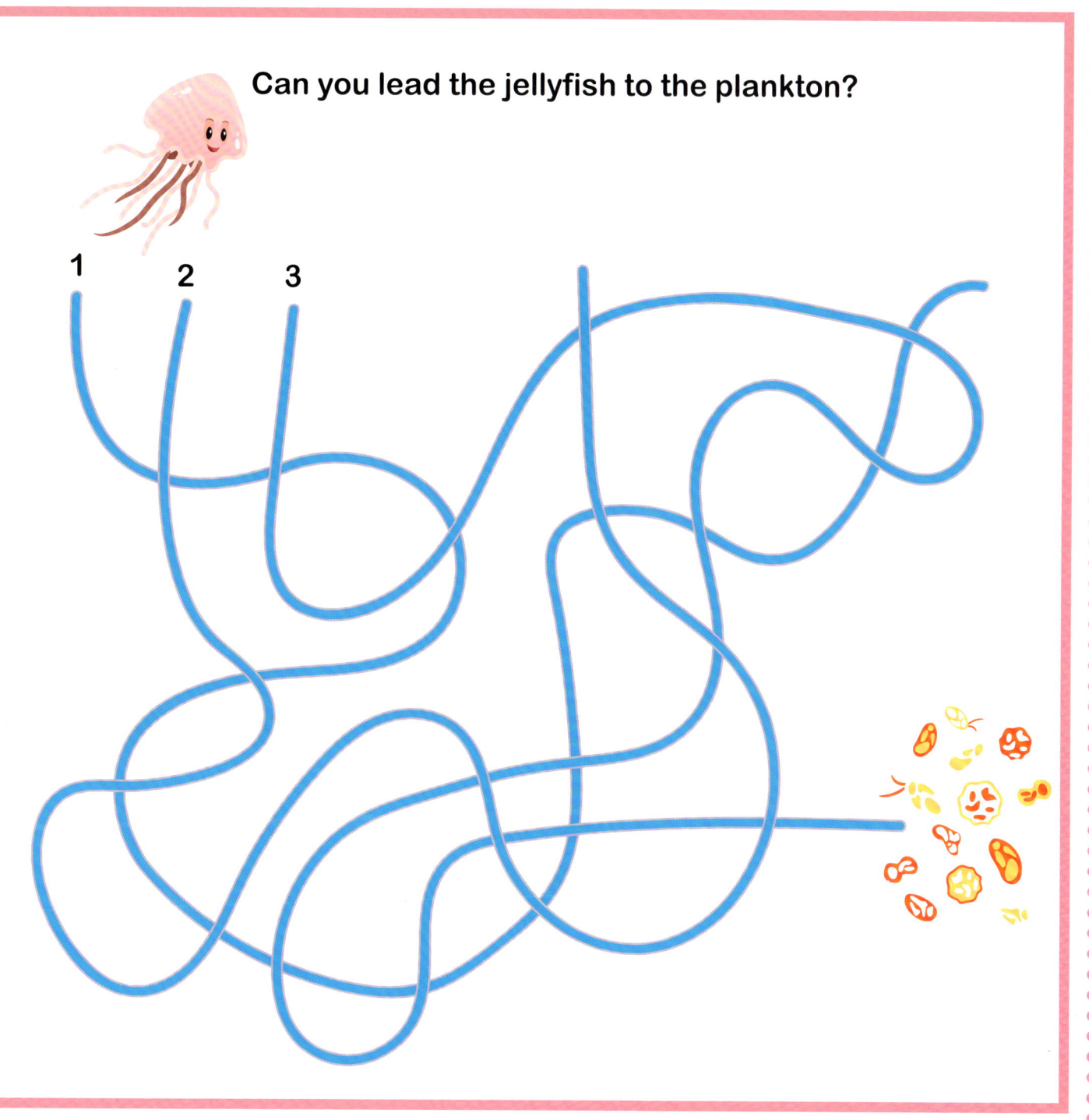

Can you fill in the missing letters?

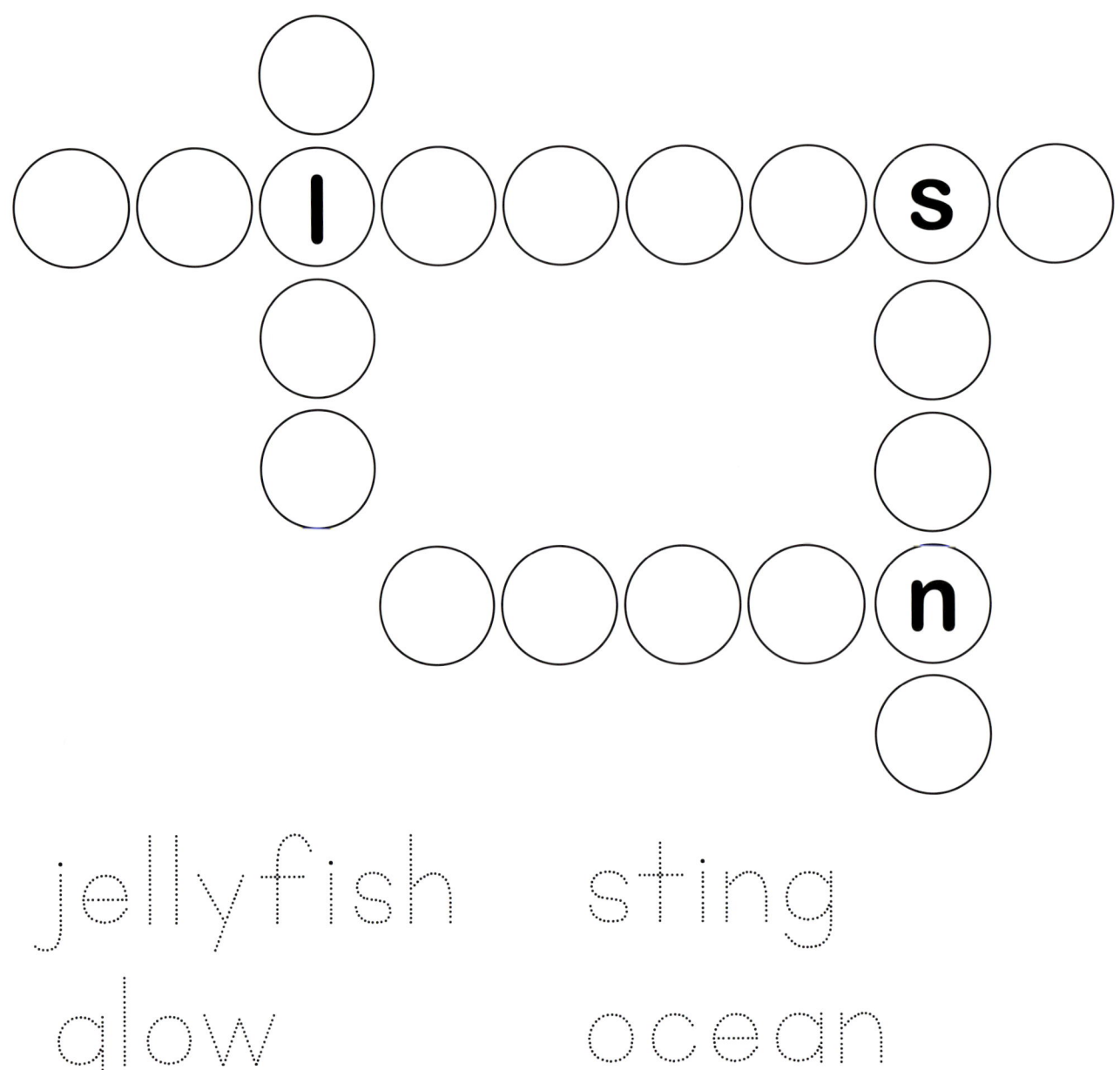

jellyfish   sting

glow   ocean

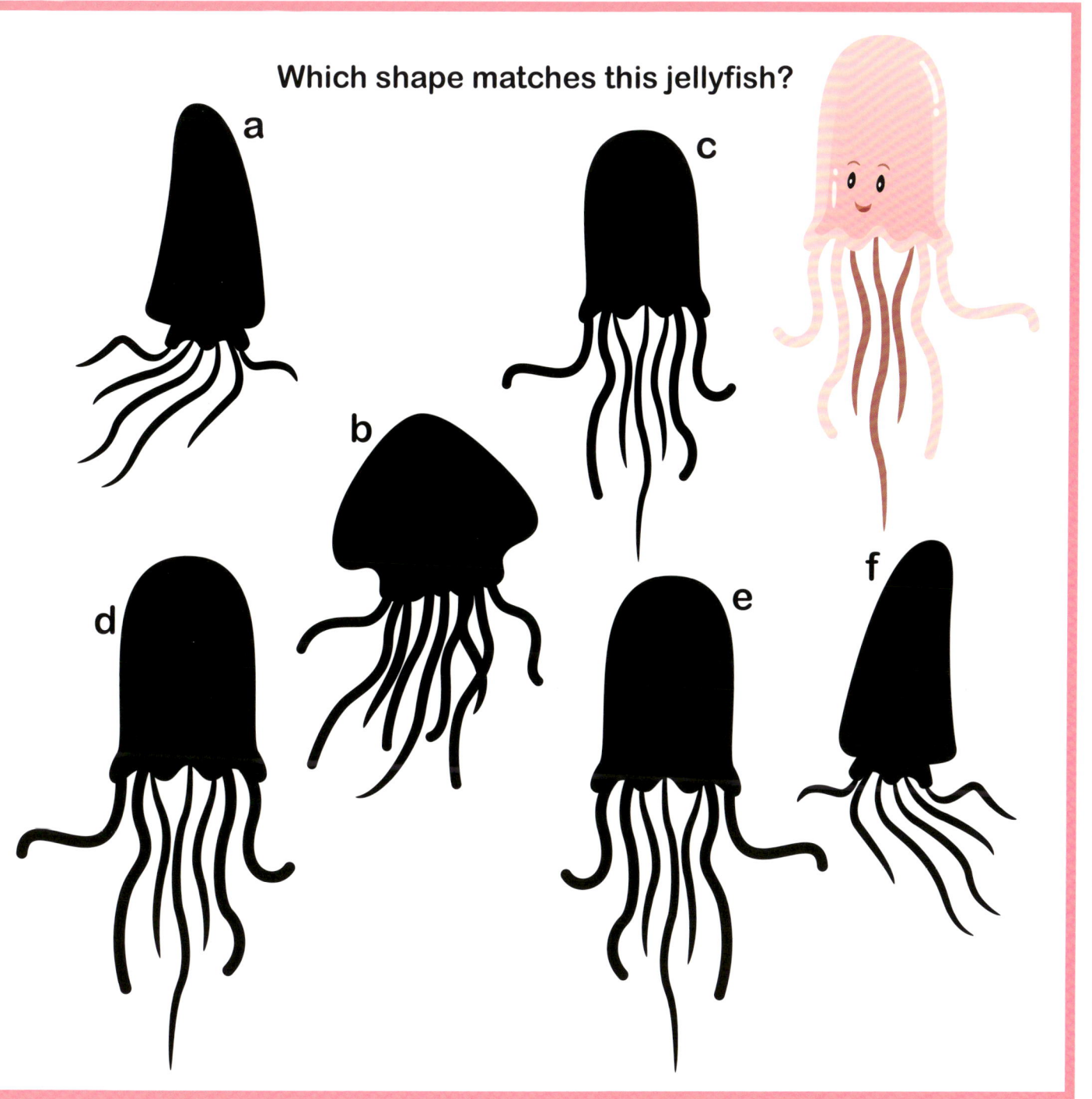

Can you find the way through the maze?

Can you complete this picture by connecting the dots?

Can you find these words?

| JELLYFISH | SEA | COLOUR | PINK |
| TENTACLES | OCEAN | STING | GREEN |

D	T	S	Y	W	B	S	H	J
J	E	L	L	Y	F	I	S	H
C	N	F	I	S	H	S	L	P
O	T	Y	E	T	K	E	O	I
L	A	H	D	I	H	A	U	Y
O	C	E	A	N	R	T	G	M
U	L	N	C	G	P	I	N	K
R	E	M	G	R	E	E	N	H
T	S	B	X	S	A	S	C	R

Can you fill in the missing words?

Jellyfish .... are long and thin.

Some jellyfish can .... in the dark.

Jellyfish eat some species of ....

Jellyfish have existed for .... of years.

plankton   tentacles   glow   millions

Can you find 7 differences?

Can you add together these jellyfish?

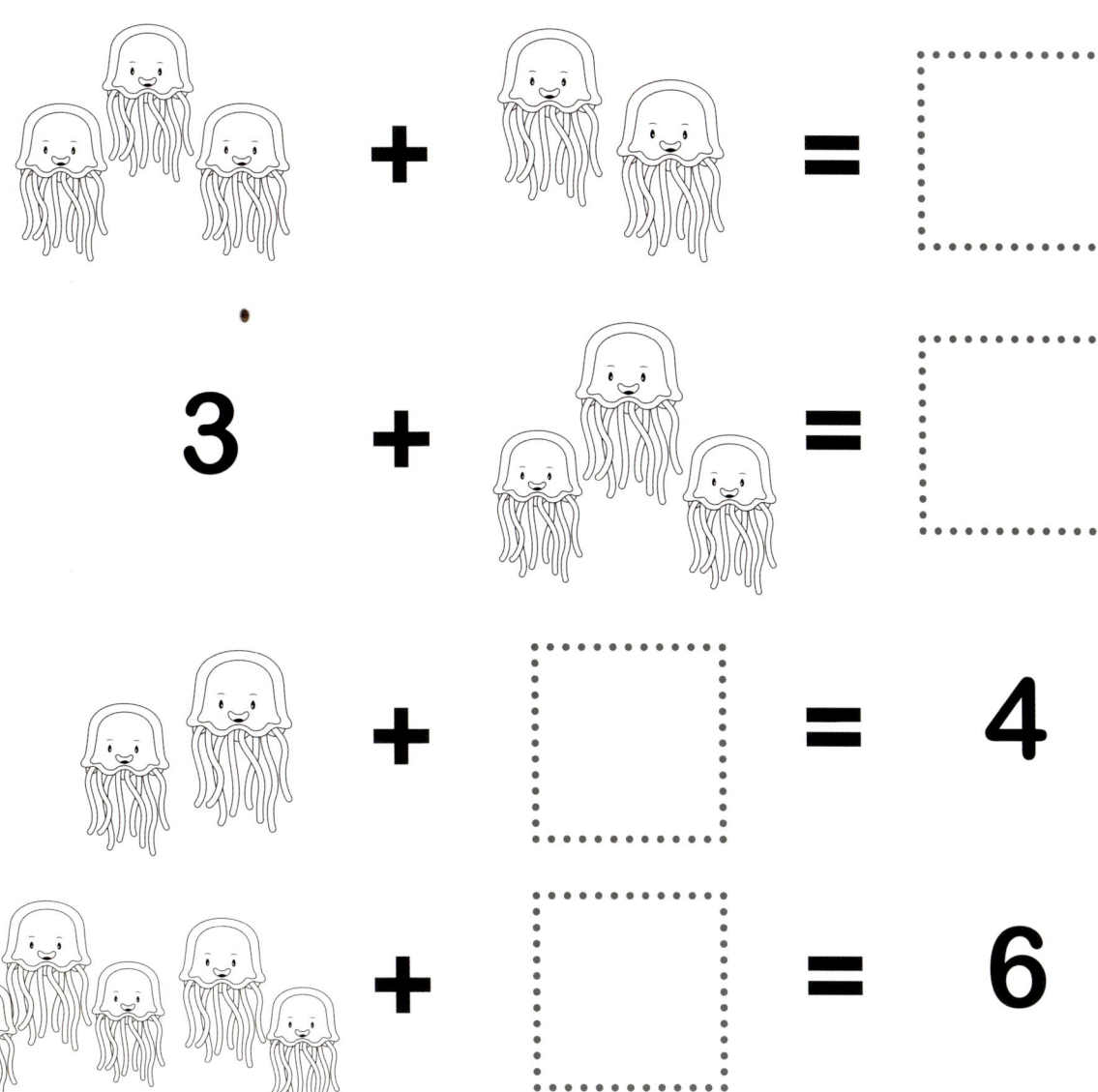

www.messyentertainment.com

Search 'Messy Entertainment'
for books, apps & much more.